Grain Brain Slow Cooker Kitchen

Top 70 Easy-To-Cook Grain Brain Slow Cooker Recipes to Help You Lose the Weight and Gain Total Health (A Low-Carb, Gluten, Sugar and Wheat Free Cookbook)

By

Betty Moore

Copyright © 2019, By: BETTY MOORE

ISBN-13: 978-1-950772-41-4
ISBN-10: 1-950772-41-1

All Rights Reserved. No part of this publication may be reproduced in any form or by any means, including scanning, photocopying, or otherwise without prior written permission of the copyright holder.

Disclaimer:

The information provided in this book is designed to provide helpful information on the subjects discussed. The publisher and author are not responsible for any specific health or allergy needs that may require medical supervision and are not liable for any damages or negative consequences from any treatment, action, application or preparation, to any person reading or following the information in this book.

Grain Brain Slow Cooker Kitchen

Table of Contents

INTRODUCTION 6

   The Grain Brain Cookbook 6

   Against All Grain 7

The Grain Brain Recipes made simple 9

   Jazzy Pork Tenderloin in Slow Cooker 9

   Slow-Cooker Apple Butter 11

   Slow Cooker Apple Sauce 13

   Slow Cooker Balsamic Mushroom and Chicken Stroganoff 15

   Slow Cooker Barbecue Pulled Chicken 17

   Slow Cooker BBQ Pulled Pork 19

   Slow Cooker Chicken and Rice Soup with a Twist 21

   Slow Cooker Chicken and Wild Rice Super Food Stew 23

   Slow Cooker Chocolate Peanut Butter Cake 25

   Slow Cooker Classic Pot Roast 27

   Slow Cooker Cornbread Stuffing 29

   Slow Cooker Cranberry Chutney 31

   Slow Cooker Fiesta Chicken Soup 33

   Slow Cooker Fudge 35

   Slow Cooker Garlic Mashed Potatoes 37

   Slow Cooker Halibut Stew 39

   Slow Cooker Herb Crusted Turkey Breast 41

   Slow Cooker Home-style Potatoes with Garlic and Rosemary 43

   Slow Cooker Honey Mustard Turkey Stew 45

   Slow Cooker Indian Chicken and Rice 47

   Slow Cooker Italian Style Penne 49

   Slow Cooker Lemon Basil Chicken with Carrots 51

   Slow Cooker Lentil and Veggie Stew 52

   Slow Cooker Lower Carb Cabbage Roll Stew 54

Slow Cooker Meatball & Potato Soup	56
Slow Cooker Mexican Meatloaf Recipe	58
Slow Cooker Monday Beans and Chicken	60
Slow Cooker Mozzarella Stuffed Meatballs	62
Slow Cooker Pomegranate Spiced Applesauce	64
Slow Cooker Pork and Beans	65
Slow Cooker Pork Tenderloin	67
Slow Cooker Pumpkin and Cranberry Topping	69
Slow Cooker Pumpkin Butter	71
Slow Cooker Rosemary Potato Soup	73
Slow Cooker Southern Style Green Beans	75
Slow Cooker Spicy Barbecued Chicken	77
Slow Cooker Spicy Sweet Potato & Bean Soup	79
Slow Cooker Spinach and Mozzarella Frittata	81
Slow Cooker Sweet Potato Mash	83
Slow Cooker Turkey Loaf	85
Slow Cooker Turkey Stew	87
Slow Cooker Turkey Stroganoff	89
Slow Cooker Winter Vegetable Medley	91
Slow Cooker Zucchini Ziti	92
Spicy Chili with Fire-Roasted Tomatoes	94
Slow Cooker Momma's Roadhouse Chili	96
Slow Cooker Thai Curry Ground Beef	98
Slow Cooker Apple Cinnamon Oatmeal	100
Slow Cooker Balsamic Chicken	102
Slow Cooker Balsamic Chicken Wrap	103
Slow Cooker Bananas Foster	104
Slow Cooker Beef Curry	105
Slow Cooker Beef Machaca *NUTRITIONAL INFORMATION*	107

- Honey Mustard Pork Roast ... 109
- Lemon Feta Vinaigrette ... 111
- Many Bean Crockpot Soup ... 112
- Mexican Crockpot Pork ... 113
- Orange Roast Pork ... 114
- Overnight Slow Cooker Pumpkin Pie Steel ... 115
- Red Potatoes with Caviar and Cheese Recipe ... 116
- Salsa Crockpot Chicken ... 118
- Saucy Crockpot Beef ... 119
- Savory Crockpot Short Ribs ... 120
- Crockpot Poached Salmon ... 121
- Shredded Asian Beef ... 122
- Slow Cooker Beef Ragu ... 124
- Slow Cooker Butter Chicken *NUTRITIONAL INFORMATION* ... 126
- Slow Cooker Butternut Squash Soup ... 128
- Slow Cooker Carnitas *NUTRITIONAL INFORMATION* ... 130
- Slow Cooker Cheesy Spaghetti with Turkey Sausage ... 132
- Slow Cooker Chicken and Mushroom Gravy ... 135

CONCLUSION ... 137
- THANK YOU. ... 138

INTRODUCTION

The Grain Brain Cookbook

Do you really know that you can change your genetic destiny to develop new brain cells? Grain Brain has significantly change the way we think about our health by uncovering the devastating effects of wheat, sugar, and carbs on the brain and has empowered us with the knowledge that what we eat is the most essential decision we make every day. If we stick to the right dieting, we can deeply affect how our brains will be working this year, next year, in five years, and for the rest of our lives.

Lifestyle strategies that promote neurogenesis and regrowth of brain cells, help you lose belly fat, lose weight and look healthy include the following:

1. You should reduce your overall calorie intake.

2. You should reduce your excess carbohydrate intake.

3. You should eat a sugar, gluten and wheat free diet.

4. You should increase healthy fat consumption in your dieting.

5. You should increase your omega-3 fat intake by eating food such as processed vegetable oils, krill oil, fish oil etc.

6. You should also engage in exercise.

Dr. David Perl mutter is not joking when he says that carbohydrates also the whole-grain carbs that we thought of as the good ones are the source of almost every modern neurologic disease. The diseases include decreased libido, chronic headaches, epilepsy, ADHD, depression, dementia, and anxiety.

It is essential to realize that, despite what the media always tells you, your brain is not "programmed" to shrink and fail as a matter of course as you get older. You should know that every activity in which you engage ranging from exercise, the foods you eat, the supplements you take, personal relationships, your emotional state, sleeping patterns. All of these factors drastically influence your genetic expression *from time to time*. Your gene is not in a static "on" or "off" position, neither are they *deterministic*.

Against All Grain

The renowned neurologist "David Perl mutter, MD", discovered the topic that is been buried in medical literature for far too long: carbs destroys your brain cells and not just unhealthy carbs, but healthy ones inclusive like whole grains can cause dementia, anxiety, ADHD, chronic headaches, depression, and much more.

Dr. Perl mutter illustrates in details what happens when the brain encounters common ingredients in your daily bread and fruit bowls, why your brain flourish on fat and cholesterol, and how you can motivate the growth of new brain cells at any age. He offers a thorough look at how we can take influence our "smart genes" through specific dietary choices and lifestyle habits, displaying how to correct our most feared diseases without drugs.

In Grain Brain, Dr. Perl mutter offers suggestions on how to fuel the brain appropriately with the right nutrition. These fundamental changes can help prevent, or even reverse brain disease, eliminate brain fog symptoms, and improve memory and energy levels.

Grain Brain went further to unfold why our brains are under siege with skyrocketing rates of dementia, ADHD, autism, depression, and much more.

Remember that if you want to boost your brain power, keep your memory, and lift your mood and energy, this book is your guide."

However, people with celiac ailment cannot tolerate gluten, not even small quantity of it. This is because a little amount of gluten in the bloodstream triggers an immune response that destroys the lining of the small intestine. This can disturb the absorption of nutrients from diet, cause a host of signs, and lead to other puzzling circumstances like osteoporosis, infertility, nerve damage, and seizures.

To abstain from gluten means more than giving up traditional breads, cereals, pasta, pizza, and beer. Gluten also concealed in many other products, ranging from frozen vegetables in sauces, soy sauce, some foods made with "natural flavorings," mineral supplements and vitamins, some medications, and even toothpaste. This has pose a challenge in following a gluten-free dieting.

According to Dr. Perl mutter, in the brain grain our immediate dietary fat phobia "has been the cornerstone of our most common degenerative diseases of the day, including Alzheimer's." the reason is because when you cut dietary fat intake and keep protein about the same, you are going to fill in the gaps with health-harming carbohydrate foods, predominantly grains.

The Grain Brain Recipes made simple

Jazzy Pork Tenderloin in Slow Cooker

NUTRITIONAL INFORMATION

Serving Size: 2 slices

Calories: 191

Fat: 4.3 g

Cholesterol: 83 mg

Sodium: 371.5 mg

Carbohydrates: 6.3 g

Dietary Fiber: 1.55 g

Protein: 30.9 g

Ingredients

1 red onion (sliced)

2 to 3 roasted or better still grilled Anaheim Chile peppers (blackened skin and seeds removed)

one can Fire-roasted, diced tomatoes in juice, or one (8-ounce) can tomato sauce

Salt, pepper, and cumin (to taste)

5 tomatillos (husked, washed, and cut in half)

5 to 6 garlic cloves (diced)

1 cup of chipotle salsa (feel free to substitute with any salsa of your choice)

1 (about 1 ½ to 2-pound) pork tenderloin roast

Directions

Meanwhile, you heat oven to a temperature of 375 degrees F.

<u>If you want to roast Chile peppers and tomatillos:</u>

1. First, you place both on a baking pan coated with a little olive oil, cut side down.
2. After which you roast for about 35 minutes.
3. After that, you remove from oven and let cool.
4. At this point when it cool, cut each 1/2 of tomatillo in 1/2 again; set aside.
5. This is when you line the bottom of slow cooker with red onion slices, and 1/2 of the diced garlic, and sprinkle with salt and pepper.
6. Then you lay the pork tenderloin roast on top of the vegetables.
7. Furthermore, you sprinkle the remainder of the diced garlic on top of the pork.
8. After which you add the roasted chills, salsa, diced tomatoes or tomato sauce, roasted tomatillos, and additional salt and pepper.
9. In addition, you sprinkle a little powdered cumin all over the top and stir gently to mix.
10. Finally, you cook on low for approximately 10 hours or until pork is tender and the meat is falling apart.

Some Serving suggestion:

You can slice or chunk pork, serve with juice, and all the vegetables on top.

Remember that Mexican rice and colorful coleslaw makes for a very healthy and tasty meal.

However, this pork would also be perfect to shred and serve in tacos.

Slow-Cooker Apple Butter

NUTRITIONAL INFORMATION

Yields: 4 half pint jars/32 servings

Serving size: 2 tablespoons

Calories: 35

Points plus: 1

Fat: 0 g

Cholesterol: 0 mg

Sodium: 56 mg

Carbohydrates: 9 g

Dietary fiber: 1 g

Sugars: 7 g

Protein: 0 g

Ingredients

3 teaspoons of cinnamon

¼ teaspoon of allspice

Pinch kosher (or sea salt)

12 medium apples (about 4 each of Granny Smith, Gala, and Honey crisp) peeled, cored, cut into 1" cubes

Note: I prefer to mix the apples with tart Granny Smith and sweet apples like Gala and Honey crisp. Other sweet apples Golden Delicious, Pink Lady, Red Delicious, Fuji, Ambrosia, and Spartan.

½ teaspoon of nutmeg

¼ teaspoon of cloves

¼ cup of unrefined sweetener, more or less to taste (recommended are: sucanat or coconut palm sugar or honey)

Directions

1. First, you combine dry ingredients in a small bowl.
2. After which you add apples to the slow-cooker, pour dry ingredients over and toss to coat.
3. Feel free to pour in honey (if you using) and stir.
4. After that, you cover, cook on low for about 8-10 hours until tender and brown (If you prefer chunky apple butter, leave as is).
5. If you want a creamier, less chunky butter, I suggest you whisk until smooth.
6. Then you allow to cool to room temperature, add to ½ pint or pint jelly jars, leave about 1" head space at the top to allow for expanding.
7. Finally, you cover with lid and freeze or refrigerate.

Slow Cooker Apple Sauce

Minimum Slow Cooker Size: about 5 quarts

NUTRITIONAL INFORMATION

Serving Size: 1/12 of the recipe

Calories: 91

Points plus: 3

Fat: 1 gm

Sodium: 2 mg

Carbohydrates: 23 gm

Dietary Fiber: 1 gm

Sugars: 19 gm

Protein: 0 gm

Ingredients

2 teaspoons of water

Pinch of nutmeg

12 Sweet Apples (some of the good choices are gala, honey crisp, pink lady or red delicious)

1 teaspoon of cinnamon

Directions

1. First, you wash apples, peel, core and slice into quarter chunks.
2. After which you place apples and water in the slow cooker.
3. After that, you cover and cook on low for about 4 hours or until desired consistency (Recommend 4-6 quart slow cooker).
4. Then you add cinnamon and nutmeg just before removing from the slow cooker.

5. Furthermore, you allow to cool completely.
6. Finally, you store in the refrigerator for up to two weeks.

Slow Cooker Balsamic Mushroom and Chicken Stroganoff

NUTRITIONAL INFORMATION

Serving Size: 1 Cup

Calories: 187

Points plus: 4

Fat: 4 gm

Sodium: 207 mg

Carbohydrates: 9 gm

Dietary fiber: 1 gm

Sugars: 5 gm

Protein: 27 gm

Ingredients

1 tablespoon of onion powder

½ lb. of brown or crimini mushrooms (sliced)

1 (about 16 oz.) container non-fat, plain Greek yogurt.

4(about 7 oz. each) raw, boneless, skinless chicken breasts

1 tablespoon of garlic powder

½ cup of balsamic vinegar

1 cup of tomato sauce (no sugar added)

Directions

1. First, you place the chicken breasts in the bottom of the slow cooker.
2. After which you sprinkle them with the onion and garlic powder

3. After that, you layer the mushrooms on top and pour the vinegar over everything.
4. Then you pour the tomato sauce over the top and cook on low for about 4-6 hours or until chicken easily falls apart.
5. Once the chicken is done, allow to cool for a bit and then stir in the Greek yogurt.

Slow Cooker Barbecue Pulled Chicken

NUTRITIONAL INFORMATION

Serving size: 3/4 cup

Calories: 237

Points plus: 6

Fat: 4 g

Sodium: 189 mg

Carbohydrates: 27 g

Dietary fiber: 0 g

Sugars: 17 g

Protein: 24 g

Ingredients

1 ½ pounds (about 4 thighs), of chicken thighs, boneless, skinless

½ teaspoon of black pepper

1 (about 18 ounce) jar barbecue sauce

1 ½ pounds (about 2 filets) of chicken breast filets, skinless

2 cups of chicken broth (fat free, low sodium)

Kosher (or preferably sea salt to taste)

Directions

1. First, you add chicken to the slow cooker, sprinkle on black pepper and pour broth over chicken.
2. After which you cover and cook on high 4 hours, or low 6 hours, until chicken shreds easily.
3. Meanwhile, you heat oven to a temperature of 350 degrees.

4. After that, you remove chicken, place in a roaster pan and shred.
5. Then you add ¼ cup of the chicken broth from slow cooker and pour barbecue sauce over chicken, coat well.
6. Finally, you cover and heat for about 15-20 minutes.
7. Make sure you serve on your favorite wheat bun or roll.
8. Remember that all chicken breasts or thighs can be used in place of half of each.

Slow Cooker BBQ Pulled Pork

NUTRITIONAL INFORMATION

Serving Size: 1/8 of entire recipe

Calories: 221

Points plus: 6

Fat: 6 g

Carbohydrates: 15 g

Sodium: 592 mg

Fiber: 1 g

Sugars: 13 g

Protein: 28 g

Ingredients

1 tablespoon of apple cider vinegar

1 tablespoon of onion powder

1 teaspoon of ground cumin

1 teaspoon of ground cinnamon

4 pork loin top loin chops

1 (about 15 ounce) can tomato sauce, no sugar added

1 tablespoon of garlic powder

¼ cup of honey

1 teaspoon of chili powder

Salt to taste

Directions

1. First, you mix together all of the ingredients in the slow cooker, except the chops (This will create the barbecue sauce).
2. However, note that this makes a lot of sauce.
3. Furthermore, if you feel it's too much, simply save some of it for another use, but do not reduce by more than half.
4. After that, you place the chops in the sauce and cook as directed.
5. Finally, you cook on low setting for about 4 to 6 hours or until the internal temperature of the meat reaches at least 165 degrees.

NOTE: meat should easily pull apart when done.

About 4-6 quart slow cooker recommended.

Slow Cooker Chicken and Rice Soup with a Twist

NUTRITIONAL INFORMATION

Serving Size: 1 Cup

Calories: 168

Points plus: 4

Fat: 5

Sodium: 339 mg

Carbohydrates: 13 g

Dietary Fiber: 1 g

Sugar: 1 g

Protein: 17 g

Ingredients

5 cups of chicken broth, fat free, low sodium (preferably homemade)

Juice of one lime

4 tablespoons of fresh cilantro (chopped)

½ teaspoon of black pepper

Salt to taste

2 cloves of minced garlic

One pound (uncooked) white and dark meat chicken, boneless, skinless (about 3 cups of cubed chicken)

2 carrots (peeled and diced)

¾ cup of long grain brown rice (uncooked)

¼ teaspoon of crushed red pepper (feel free to add more for a spicier soup)

Directions

1. First, you cut chicken into 1" cubes and remove any visible fat.
2. After which you add uncooked chicken cubes and all other ingredients to the slow-cooker.
3. Then you cook on low heat for about 6-8 hours or until rice is tender and chicken is cooked through.

Slow Cooker Chicken and Wild Rice Super Food Stew

NUTRITIONAL INFORMATION

1 Serving Size = 1/2 cup

Calories: 88

Points plus: 2

Fat: 2 gm

Sodium: 110 mg

Carbohydrates: 8 gm

Dietary fiber: 2 gm

Sugars: 1 gm

Protein: 10 gm

Ingredients

¼ cup of chopped white/yellow onion

4 cups of fresh spinach (tightly packed)

½ lb. of broccoli

4 cubes of vegetable bouillon (with no added salt)

4 cups of chicken broth

1 (about 15 oz.) can kidney beans

   4 medium carrots (chopped)

½ cup of dry wild rice

½ lb. of crimini mushrooms

2 cloves of garlic (minced)

4 chicken breast fillets (make sure you add raw chicken cut into 2" chunks)

1(about 28 oz.) can diced tomatoes, with juice

Directions

1. First, you add ingredients to the slow cooker in the following order. For example, place carrots on the bottom, followed by rice, spinach, mushrooms, broccoli, garlic, vegetable bouillon, chicken, tomatoes and finally beans.
2. Then you cover and cook on low for about 6-8 hours.

Slow Cooker Chocolate Peanut Butter Cake

NUTRITIONAL INFORMATION

Serving Size: 1 Slice

Calories: 141

Points plus: 3

Fat: 3 g

Carbohydrates: 19 g

Fiber: 3 g

Sugars: 10 g

Protein: 3 g

Ingredients

1 tablespoon of baking powder

2 egg whites

2 teaspoons of pure vanilla extract

¾ cup of unsweetened apple sauce

1 cup of whole wheat pastry flour

½ cup of honey (optional coconut palm sugar)

1/3 cup of peanut butter, no sugar added (remember that additional peanut butter will be needed if you wish to ice the cake with it)

½ cup of unsweetened cocoa powder

Directions

1. First, you line the bottom of your slow cooker with cut-to-fit parchment paper and spray the inside using an oil sprayer.

2. After which in a large mixing bowl, you whisk together the flour, cocoa powder and baking powder until well combined.
3. Then in a second large mixing bowl, you whisk together all your wet ingredients including the peanut butter, and then combine the two bowls.
4. Finally, you stir all ingredients together until well combined.
5. Cook on low for about 4 hours, or until a knife inserted in the middle pulls out clean

Slow Cooker Classic Pot Roast

I Recommend 6 quart slow cooker.

NUTRITIONAL INFORMATION

Serving Size: 1 Cup

Calories: 402

Points plus: 11

Fat: 26 gm (This will vary based on the meat you choose)

Sodium: 239 mg

Carbohydrates: 13 gm

Dietary Fiber: 2 gm

Sugars: 1 gm

Protein: 29 gm

Ingredients

2 medium red potatoes, should be sliced into wedges (8 small red potatoes, it is optional)

2 bay leaves

3 cloves garlic (minced)

2 cups of beef broth, fat free, low sodium

½ teaspoon of black pepper

2 tablespoons of water (it is optional)

3 large carrots, peeled and sliced (2 cups of baby carrots, optional)

1 medium onion (sliced thinly)

One (about 3 pound) boneless chuck roast or better still tenderloin for an extra lean cut

1 tablespoon of balsamic vinegar

Kosher (or preferably sea salt to taste)

2 tablespoons of cornstarch or Tapioca starch (it is optional)

Directions

1. First, you add carrots, potatoes, onion, bay leaves, roast, garlic, vinegar and broth to slow cooker, in that order.
2. After which you sprinkle with salt and pepper, cover and cook on low for about 6-8 hours or until internal temperature of roast has reached 145 degrees and vegetables are tender.
3. If using a Set'n forget slow cooker, I suggest you set the internal temperature of the roast to reach 145 degrees.
4. Then for a thicker gravy, I suggest you combine cornstarch and water, pour into slow cooker the last 15 minutes of cooking time, for a thicker sauce.

Slow Cooker Cornbread Stuffing

NUTRITIONAL INFORMATION

Serving: 1/10th of recipe

Calories: 171

Points plus: 5

Fat: 6 g

Sodium: 263 mg

Carbohydrates: 26 g

Dietary Fiber: 1 g

Sugars: 4 g

Protein: 4 g

Ingredients

1 cup of diced celery (about 6 stalks)

6-7 cups of cornbread crumbs (Old-fashion Cornbread recipe)

½ teaspoon of black pepper

Kosher (or better still sea salt to taste)

2 tablespoons of Extra Virgin Olive Oil

1 yellow onion (diced)

2 teaspoons of poultry seasoning

2 cups of chicken broth (fat free, low sodium)

Directions

1. First, you add oil in a large skillet and cook celery and onion on medium-low heat until tender, about 4 minutes.

2. After which you combine in a large mixing bowl cornbread crumbs, black pepper and salt.
3. After that, you add all remaining ingredients to cornbread mixture, stir well.
4. At this point, you lightly spray the inside of slow cooker with non-stick cooking spray.
5. Then you add cornbread mixture and spread evenly.
6. Furthermore, you cover and cook on low for 4 hours (NOTE: Recommend 5-6 quart slow cooker).
7. If you want an additional browning, I suggest you pre-heat oven to broil, use oven mitts and remove, oven safe, slow cooker insert, place on the middle oven rack.
8. Finally, you broil for about 5 - 8 minutes or until desired color is reached.

Tip:

You can substitute whole grain bread crumbs for cornbread crumbs or combine the two for an equally yummy stuffing.

Slow Cooker Cranberry Chutney

I recommend you use a minimum Slow Cooker size: 4 quarts

NUTRITIONAL INFORMATION

Serving Size: ¼ Cup

Points plus: 2

Calories: 62

Fat: 0 g

Carbohydrates: 17 g

Sugars: 14 g

Fiber: 2 g

Sodium: 1 mg

Protein: 0 g

Ingredients

1 Gala apple (peeled, cored and diced)

1 teaspoon of freshly grated ginger

½ cup of mild honey

1 (about 12 ounce) bag fresh cranberries, rinsed

2 cinnamon sticks

1 tablespoon of Apple Cider vinegar

¼ cup of 100% orange juice

Directions

1. First, you add all the above ingredients to the slow cooker, stir (I Recommend you use 3-5 quart slow cooker).
2. After which you cover and cook on low for 3 hours.

3. Then you remove cinnamon sticks, allow to cool and store in the refrigerator in a glass container with lid.

Slow Cooker Fiesta Chicken Soup

NUTRITIONAL INFORMATION

Serving size: 1 cup

Calories: 192

Points plus: 4

Fat: 3 g

Sodium: 202 mg

Carbohydrates: 21 g

Dietary fiber: 6 g

Sugars: 2 g

Protein: 20 g

Ingredients

1 clove garlic (minced)

1 (about 15 oz.) can kidney beans (rinsed and drained)

1 (about 14.5 oz.) can diced tomatoes

1 cup of frozen (or better still fresh corn)

1 tablespoon of chili powder

½ teaspoon of cayenne pepper (more or less to taste)

Kosher (or preferably sea salt to taste)

2 chicken breasts fillets, skinless, cut into 1-2" cubes (there is no need to pre-cook)

½ cup of diced onion

1 (about 15 oz.) can black beans, rinsed and drained

1 (about 4.5 oz.) can diced green chili peppers

2 ½ cups of chicken broth, low sodium, fat-free (you can use more broth for a thinner soup)

Juice from one lime

1 teaspoon of cumin

½ teaspoon of black pepper

½ cup of freshly cilantro (chopped)

Directions

1. First, you add all ingredients to the slow cooker, stir to combine.
2. After which you cover and cook on low for 6-8 hours.

Slow Cooker Fudge

NUTRITIONAL INFORMATION

Serving Size: 1 piece of fudge

Calories: 114 g

Points plus: 3

Fat: 8 g

Sodium: 21 mg

Carbohydrates: 17 g

Sugars: 10 g

Dietary Fiber: 1 g

Protein: 1 g

Ingredients

½ cup of coconut milk, (make sure it is canned, and not in a carton)

Dash of sea salt

1 teaspoon of pure vanilla extract

2-1/2 cups of Chocolate Chips, [I prefer to use dark chocolate chips because of their health benefits. Ghirardelli is a good brand and works well with this recipe)

¼ cup of coconut sugar (optional honey or better still maple syrup)

2 tablespoons of coconut oil

Directions

1. Remember fudge is perfect for the slow cooker because it doesn't scorch or burn.
2. First, you add chocolate chips, coconut milk, coconut sugar, salt, and coconut oil, stir to combine.
3. After which you cover and cook on low for about 2 hours without stirring (NOTE: It's important that lid remain on during the 2 hours).
4. Then after 2 hours, you turn the slow cooker off, uncover, and add vanilla (NOTE: Do not stir fudge mixture at this point).

5. At this point, you allow to cool to room temperature, or it reaches 110 degrees with a candy thermometer.
6. Furthermore, once cooled, you use a large spoon, stir vigorously for about 5-10 minutes until it loses some the gloss.
7. After that, you oil lightly an 8"x8" square pan.
8. Finally, you pour fudge into pan, cover and refrigerate for about 4 hours or until firm (**NOTE:** This fudge is very rich and meant to be eaten on occasion as a treat).

Tip:

You can find canned coconut milk in the Asian or preferably organic sections of most grocery stores.

Slow Cooker Garlic Mashed Potatoes

NUTRITIONAL INFORMATION

Serving Size: 1/2 Cup

Calories: 144

Points plus: 4

Fat: 1 gm

Sodium: 37 mg

Carbohydrates: 28 gm

Dietary fiber: 2 gm

Sugars: 3 gm

Protein: 5 gm

Ingredients

½ cup of low sodium chicken broth (with no sugar added)

1 tablespoon of olive oil

Salt to taste

3 lb. of russet potatoes

10 cloves garlic (chopped)

1 cup of non-fat, plain yogurt (preferably Greek yogurt)

½ cup of 1% milk (or preferably more for consistency)

Directions

1. First, you prep your potatoes as usual by washing and cutting out any bad spots.
2. After which you puncture holes in the potatoes with a fork (be careful so you don't stab yourself!)

3. After that, you place all the potatoes in the microwave for about 15 minutes on high or until they are nearly fully cooked.
4. Apply caution when removing them from the microwave, they will be HOT (we learned this the hard way. Ouch!)
5. At this point, you allow potatoes to cool enough to be able to handle them.
6. Then while they are in the microwave, you sauté the garlic in the olive oil for about 2-3 minutes.
7. Furthermore, you cut cooled potatoes into slices and place in slow cooker with chicken broth.
8. After that, you pour the garlic on top of that and mix everything up briefly to distribute.
9. In addition, you cook on low for about 1 to 1-1/2 hours or until the potatoes are completely cooked and soft.
10. This is when you remove the insert from the heating element with pot holders and place on a heat-safe surface.
11. Finally, you use a hand blender or potato masher, mash the potatoes together with the milk and yogurt.
12. Then you add salt to taste.

Slow Cooker Halibut Stew

NUTRITIONAL INFORMATION

Serving size: 1 cup

Calories: 148

Points plus: 3

Fat: 2 g

Sodium: 296 mg

Carbohydrates: 12 g

Dietary fiber: 2 g

Sugars: 4 g

Protein: 18 g

Ingredients

1 small yellow onion (coarsely chopped)

1 large potato (peeled, cut into 1" pieces)

Juice from one lime

½ teaspoon of black pepper

1 teaspoon of chili powder

½ teaspoon of cumin

1 pound of halibut fillets, rinsed and cut into bite size pieces (or, better still your favorite white fish as an option)

1 red bell pepper (diced)

2 carrots (thinly sliced)

1 ½ cups of chicken broth, fat free, low sodium (vegetable broth, optional)

2 cloves of garlic

Kosher (or preferably sea salt to taste)

¼ cup of freshly chopped cilantro

½ teaspoon of red pepper flakes

Directions

1. First, you add all the above ingredients to the slow-cooker, except halibut.
2. After which you cover and cook on low for about 8 to 9 hours.
3. Furthermore, the last 30 minutes of cooking time you add thawed halibut pieces.
4. Then you garnish with additional cilantro if desired (NOTE: Recommend 4-6 quart slow-cooker).

Slow Cooker Herb Crusted Turkey Breast

NUTRITIONAL INFORMATION

Serving Size: 1/6 of the finished recipe

Calories: 233

Points plus: 5

Fat: 3 gm

Sodium: 119 mg

Carbohydrates: 4 gm

Dietary Fiber: 1 gm

Sugars: 1 gm

Protein: 45 gm

Ingredients

1 tablespoon of garlic powder

1 teaspoon of dried thyme

1 tablespoon of onion powder

2 ½ lb. of turkey breast (on the bone and had skin that we removed before eating)

1 tablespoon of poultry seasoning

¼ teaspoon of black pepper

Directions

1. First, you mix all the spices together in a small mixing bowl.
2. After which you place your turkey breast on a plate and cover both sides with spices (**NOTE:** It should be completely coated in spice mix).
3. Then you place in slow cooker (no liquid) and cook as directed (NOTE: Recommend 5-7 quart slow cooker).

4. Cook on low for 4-5 hours or until it reaches at least 165 degrees F. on a meat thermometer.

Slow Cooker Home-style Potatoes with Garlic and Rosemary

NUTRITIONAL INFORMATION

Calories: 179

Fat: 9 g

Points plus: 9

Sodium: 6 mg

Carbohydrates: 23 g

Dietary Fiber: 2 g

Sugars: 1 g

Protein: 2 g

Ingredients

4 medium red potatoes, cubed into 1/2" pieces (preferably unpeeled)

1 tablespoon of chopped fresh rosemary

Kosher (or preferably sea salt to taste)

¼ cup of extra virgin olive oil (note evoo is a good fat)

3 cloves garlic (minced)

½ teaspoon of black pepper

Directions

1. First, you add oil to the slow cooker, turn to high and allow to heat up while preparing potatoes (about 15 minutes of preheating is good).
2. After which you combine all ingredients in the slow cooker, toss potatoes in oil, cover and cook on high for about 2-3 hours (4-5 hours on low), or until potatoes are tender and browned.
3. I recommend you use 5 - 7 quart slow cooker.
4. Remember that the fats in this recipe are from heart healthy extra-virgin olive oil.

Slow Cooker Honey Mustard Turkey Stew

NUTRITIONAL INFORMATION

Serving Size: 1 cup

Points plus: 5

Calories: 211

Fat: 1 g

Carbohydrates: 14 g

Sugars: 7 g

Fiber: 2.3 g

Sodium: 240 mg

Protein: 33.3 g

Ingredients

1 ½ cups of celery (chopped)

1 cup of chicken broth (with no salt added)

1 teaspoon of dried rosemary

2 Tablespoons of spelt flour (or preferably whole wheat flour for gluten free I suggest you use oat or brown rice flour)

1 cup of carrots (chopped)

1 ½ cups of onions (chopped)

2 Tablespoons of honey

2 Tablespoons of grainy Dijon mustard

1 large turkey breast (make sure you cut into chunks)

Directions

1. First, you toss cut up turkey breast in flour to coat.
2. After which you place everything in slow cooker and stir.
3. After that, you cover and cook on low for about 6-8 hours or high for 3-4 hours.

Slow Cooker Indian Chicken and Rice

NUTRITIONAL INFORMATION

Serving Size: 3/4 cup

Calories: 254

Points plus: 6

Fat: 4

Sodium: 307 mg

Carbohydrates: 34 g

Sugars: 3 g

Dietary Fiber: 3 g

Protein: 18 g

Ingredients

1 cup of long grain brown rice (uncooked)

2 cups of chicken broth (fat free, low sodium)

¼ teaspoon of ginger

¼ teaspoon of cloves

½ teaspoon of cayenne pepper

1 teaspoon of chili powder

1 teaspoon of curry

Salt to taste

4 tablespoons of fresh mint leaves

2 cloves garlic (minced)

3 chicken breasts (about 2 lbs.), skinless, boneless, cut into 1" strips

½ cup of Greek Yogurt (low fat, plain)

1 (about 4 oz.) can Green Chile Peppers (drained and diced)

¼ teaspoon of cinnamon

¼ teaspoon of turmeric

1 teaspoon of black pepper

1 teaspoon of coriander

1 teaspoon of paprika

1 Bay Leaf

1 tablespoon of Extra Virgin olive oil

1 medium onion (cut into thin rings)

Directions

1. First, in a medium skillet you add 1 tablespoon of Extra Virgin olive oil and sauté onion and garlic on medium heat, cook for about 5 minutes or until onion is tender.
2. After which you set aside 2 tablespoons of mint leaves for garnish and 5-6 sautéed onion rings for garnish.
3. Then in a large mixing bowl, you add sautéed onion and garlic, all other spices and herbs, Greek yogurt, chicken broth and chicken strips; stir to thoroughly coat chicken.
4. After that, you cover and place chicken mixture in the refrigerator for about 1-2 hours, allowing the flavors time to meld.
5. At this point, you turn slow cooker to high.
6. This is when you add rice (uncooked) on the bottom of the slow cooker.
7. Furthermore, you add chicken mixture over rice, cover and cook on high for about 3-4 hours or low for 5-6.
8. After that, you check after 2 hours two hours to see if additional liquid is needed…if so, add another 1/2 cup chicken broth.
9. Then you cook until chicken is cooked through and rice is tender, remove bay leaf.
10. Finally, you garnish with remaining mint leaves and onion rings and a few raisins if desired.

Slow Cooker Italian Style Penne

NUTRITIONAL INFORMATION

Serving Size: 1 Cup

Calories: 293

Points plus: 5

Fat: 8 gm

Sodium: 190 mg

Carbohydrates: 22 gm

Dietary fiber: 4 gm

Sugars: 3 gm

Protein: 6 gm

Ingredients

1 (about 15 oz.) can kidney beans, with no sugar added (drained and rinsed)

1 teaspoon of Italian herb seasoning

1 teaspoon of onion powder

Parmesan cheese (for garnish)

1 (about 28 oz.) or 2 (about 14.5 oz.) can(S) diced tomatoes, low or no sodium

½ pound dry, whole wheat penne pasta

1 teaspoon of garlic powder

½ cup of low sodium, chicken or better still vegetable broth, with no sugar added

Balsamic Vinegar (to taste)

Directions

1. However, for this recipe, you will want to layer your ingredients.
2. First, you place the pasta on the bottom of your slow cooker insert.
3. After which on top of that, pour the diced tomatoes.
4. After that, you add the beans.
5. Furthermore, you pour the broth over the top.
6. Then you sprinkle the Italian herb seasoning, garlic and onion powder over the top and cook on low for 1-1/2 to 2 hours, or until pasta is cooked to your liking.
7. Remember that it's okay to lift the lid on this one to check.
8. At this point when finished, you add a splash of balsamic vinegar to taste.
9. Finally, you top with a small amount of freshly grated parmesan cheese.

Slow Cooker Lemon Basil Chicken with Carrots

NUTRITIONAL INFORMATION

Serving Size: 3/4 cup

Calories: 165

Points plus: 4

Fat: 5 g

Sodium: 79 mg

Carbohydrates: 3 g

Dietary fiber: 1 g

Sugars: 1 g

Protein: 26 g

Ingredients

¼ cup of chicken broth (with no sugar added)

4 medium carrots (peeled and thinly sliced)

5 raw, boneless, skinless chicken breast (about 8 oz. each)

¼ cup of fresh squeezed lemon juice (about 2 lemons)

1 tablespoons of dry basil

Directions

1. First, you place the carrots in the bottom of the slow cooker and put everything else on top of them.
2. After which you cook on low for about 4-5 hours, or until chicken reaches an internal temperature of at least 165 degrees F.
3. Remember the chicken should shred easily when it's done.
4. Finally, you shred chicken and serve by itself or over whole grains of choice.

Slow Cooker Lentil and Veggie Stew

NUTRITIONAL INFORMATION

Serving size: 1 1/2 cups

Calories: 221

Points plus: 5

Fat: 2 g

Sodium: 312 mg

Carbohydrates: 42 g

Dietary fiber: 11 g

Sugars: 7 g

Protein: 11 g

Ingredients

1 large red potato (cut into 1" cubes)

½ cup of diced sweet onion

1 cup (fresh or preferably frozen) green beans, broken into 1" pieces

½ teaspoon of black pepper

1 ½ cups of tomato juice, low sodium (V-8 Juice low-sodium, optional)

1 cup (dry) lentils

1 cup whole kernel corn (frozen or fresh)

4 carrots (sliced)

2 stalks celery (sliced into 1/2" pieces)

½ teaspoon of paprika

Kosher (or better still sea salt to taste)

3 cups of vegetable broth, low sodium (chicken broth, optional)

Directions

1. First, you add all of the above ingredients, except lentils, to the slow cooker, stir to combine.
2. After which you cover and cook on low for about 8 to 10 hours.
3. After that, you add lentils the last hour of cooking time.
4. You can add or substitute your favorite vegetables.

Tip:

1. Make sure you adjust the liquid for less or more thickness.
2. First you try adding 1 cup of each tomato juice and 1 cup vegetable broth.
3. Note that the slow cooker does not allow for much evaporation, so the amount of liquid you add initially will be about the same toward the end of the cooking cycle.
4. Remember, it's easier to add liquid than to remove it.
5. I prefer mine to be fairly juicy so I add the full amount and sometimes even more.
6. I recommend you use a minimum slow cooker size of 4 quarts.

Slow Cooker Lower Carb Cabbage Roll Stew

NUTRITIONAL INFORMATION

Serving Size: 1 1/3 Cup

Calories: 242

Points plus: 6

Fat: 13 g

Carbohydrates: 14 g

Fiber: 3 g

Sugars: 6 g

Protein: 17 g

Ingredients

1 (about 14oz) can low sodium (or better still no salt added) tomato sauce

1 pound extra lean ground beef (feel free to also use ground bison or moose)

1 Tablespoon of minced garlic

½ teaspoon of hot chili flakes

½ head cabbage (chopped)

1 medium onion (chopped)

1 Tablespoon of Worcestershire sauce

1 (about 14.5 oz.) can stewed tomatoes

1 cup of low sodium chicken broth (or beef broth)

1 teaspoon of black pepper

Directions

1. First, in a medium pot, you brown beef and onions.
2. After which you place everything in slow cooker (except meat mixture and cabbage) and mix well.
3. Then you add beef mixture, then cabbage.
4. Finally, you cook on LOW for 5-6 hours.

Slow Cooker Meatball & Potato Soup

NUTRITIONAL INFORMATION

Serving Size: 1 cup or 1/6th of recipe

Calories: 234

Points plus: 6

Fat: 11 g

Carbohydrates: 17 g

Dietary Fiber: 2 g

Sugars: 6 g

Protein: 19 g

Ingredients

Ingredients for the Soup:

1 cup of diced yellow onion

1 (large) Yukon Gold potato (cut into 1" cubes)

½ teaspoon of black pepper

1 cup of chicken broth (fat-free, low sodium)

1 tablespoon of cornstarch (it is optional)

2 cups of kale leaves, (stems removed) rinsed and coarsely chopped

1 tablespoon of extra-virgin olive oil

1 clove garlic (minced)

½ teaspoon of red pepper flakes

1 teaspoon of salt

2 cups 1% milk

1 tablespoon of cold milk (it is optional)

Ingredients for the Meatballs:

¼ teaspoon of Kosher (or better still sea salt)

½ teaspoon of crushed red pepper flakes

1/8 teaspoon of allspice

1 pound of lean ground chicken

½ teaspoon of black pepper

½ teaspoon of chili powder

Directions

1. First, you combine in a medium bowl meatball ingredients and shape into 1" bite size meatballs.
2. After which you cover and place in the refrigerator.
3. Then in a medium skillet sauté onion over medium-low heat about 4 minutes until tender.
4. After that, you add garlic and sauté for 1 minute.
5. Furthermore, in the same skillet add the meatballs and lightly brown on the outside over medium heat, drain fat
6. Remember that the meatballs needn't be cooked through all the way, but just evenly browned on the outside.
7. At this point, you add to slow cooker, meatballs, sautéed onion, garlic, potato cubes, red pepper flakes, black pepper, salt, chicken broth and milk, and stir just to combine.
8. After which you cover and cook on low for about 6 to 8 hours.
9. Finally, you add kale and cook for about 10 -15 minutes until wilted.

Optional:

If you want a thicker soup, I suggest you combine cornstarch and cold milk, stir until smooth and add to slow cooker the last 20 minutes of cooking time.

Slow Cooker Mexican Meatloaf Recipe

NUTRITIONAL INFORMATION

Serving Size: 1 2-inch thick slice

Calories: 335

Points plus: 9

Fat: 18 g

Sodium: 534 mg

Carbohydrates: 12 g

Dietary Fiber: 2 g

Sugars: 5 g

Protein: 30 g

Ingredients

Ingredients for the Meatloaf:

1 onion (chopped)

1 clove garlic (minced)

1 teaspoon of ground cumin

½ teaspoon of sea salt

1 egg

2 tablespoons of olive oil

1 jalapeño (minced)

1 pound ground beef

¼ teaspoon of cayenne pepper

¼ teaspoon of black pepper

½ cup of rolled oats (coarsely ground in a food processor)

Ingredients for the Glaze:

1 clove garlic (minced)

1 tablespoon of lime juice

¼ teaspoon of sea salt

1 cup of diced tomatoes in juice

1 tablespoon of honey

1 canned chipotle chili in adobo sauce

Directions

1. First, you heat a skillet over medium heat.
2. After which you add the olive oil, onions, and jalapeño.
3. After that, you cook until soft and add the garlic.
4. Then you cook for 1 minute and add to a large bowl.
5. At this point, you stir in the beef and seasonings and mix well.
6. Once mixture is slightly cool, you add the oats and egg and mix well.
7. This is when you shape the mixture into a round loaf and transfer to a slow cooker pot.
8. Furthermore, you cover and cook on low, for about 6 hours.
9. Then before you serve, you make the glaze by combining all of the ingredients in a small saucepan.
10. After which you bring to a boil, cook for about 5 minutes and transfer to a blender.
11. Make sure you blend until smooth.
12. Finally, you spoon over the meatloaf before serving.

Slow Cooker Monday Beans and Chicken

Minimum slow cooker size: 4 quarts

NUTRITIONAL INFORMATION

1 Serving: 1/2 Cup

Calories: 129

Points plus: 3

Fat: 2 g

Carbohydrates: 13

Dietary Fiber: 3 g

Sugars: 2 g

Protein: 16 g

Ingredients

1 pound of chicken breasts

(NOTE: If you don't want to use meat, I suggest you increase some spices to taste)

2 or 3 tablespoons of minced garlic

½ teaspoon of sea salt

2 bay leaves

I pound of your favorite dried beans (remember 10 bean soup will work too) soaked over night

1 pound of combined, chopped onion, bell pepper (feel free to use any color) and celery

2 teaspoons of cayenne pepper

½ teaspoon of black pepper

2 tablespoons of parsley flakes

Directions

1. First, you put all in slow cooker and cover with low fat, low sodium chicken broth cook on low for about 7 hours.
2. Then if thicker broth is desired, you use a spoon to mash up some beans against the side of the pot.
3. After that, you serve over brown rice or as a soup.
4. Remember that this recipe can easily be cut in half (simply cut all ingredients by half).

Slow Cooker Mozzarella Stuffed Meatballs

NUTRITIONAL INFORMATION

Serving size: 3 meatballs

Calories: 255

Fat: 14 g

Points plus: 7

Sodium: 153 mg

Carbohydrates: 12 g

Dietary Fiber: 3 g

Sugars: 3 g

Protein: 21 g

Ingredients

1 medium onion, divided (finely chopped)

1 large egg

½ teaspoon of black pepper

Whole-wheat flour to coat the meatballs

½ cup of chicken broth

4 fresh sage leaves (roughly chopped)

1 pound lean ground turkey

1 slice whole grain bread (lightly toasted and ground)

1 teaspoon of Kosher (or better still sea salt, divided)

1 (about 3.5-ounce) ball of mozzarella (roughly chopped)

Extra-virgin olive oil (for browning)

1 (about 14-ounce) can diced tomatoes

1 teaspoon of dried oregano

Directions

1. First, you mix in a medium bowl turkey, ground bread crumbs, egg, half of the onions, ½ teaspoon salt and black pepper.
2. After which you mix well until it becomes compact.
3. After that, you make a small balls then push a few pieces of the mozzarella at the center of each meatball.
4. At this point, you roll the meatballs on a plate with flour then set aside.
5. Then over medium heat, in a saucepan with olive oil, brown the outside of the meatballs.
6. Once they are browned, you set them aside in a bowl.
7. This is when you discard the oil (Note: the meatballs do not need to be cooked through all the way as they will cook in the sauce and slow cooker).
8. Furthermore, over medium heat, still in the same saucepan, you pour some new oil then sauté the remaining onion.
9. After which you put back the meatballs then pour in the broth.
10. Then you cook until the sauce thickens.
11. Finally, in the slow cooker, you pour the meatballs with the sauce, canned tomatoes, oregano, sage, the remaining salt and a dash of pepper.
12. After that, you set the slow cooker too low for about 6 hours or high for 4 hours.

Slow Cooker Pomegranate Spiced Applesauce

NUTRITIONAL INFORMATION

Calories: 73

Points plus: 3

Fat: 1 g

Carbohydrate: 23 g

Dietary Fiber: 3 g

Sugars: 32 g

Protein: 0 g

Ingredients

2 whole cloves

¼ cup of sucanat, coconut palm sugar or better still honey

½ cup of 100% pomegranate juice (with no sugar added)

4 Granny Smith Apples (peeled and cored)

1 teaspoon of cinnamon

1 teaspoon of lemon juice

Directions

1. First, you slice apples into quarters and add to the slow cooker along with the remaining ingredients.
2. After which you cover and cook on low for about 6 to 8 hours or until apples are chunk consistency.

NOTE: I recommend you use 4-5 quart slow cooker.

Then you remove cloves and serve.

Slow Cooker Pork and Beans

NUTRITIONAL INFORMATION

Serving Size: 1 cup

Calories: 243

Points plus: 7

Fat: 5 gm

Sodium: 557 mg

Carbohydrates: 19 gm

Dietary fiber: 3 gm

Sugars: 6 gm

Protein: 31 gm

Ingredients

2 (about 15 oz.) cans pinto beans with their liquid (please do not drain)

½ cup of naturally sweetened ketchup (I prefer the Organic Ville brand)

1 tablespoon of apple cider vinegar

3 lb. of pork loin chops

¼ cup of molasses (unsulfured)

1 teaspoon of garlic powder

1 tablespoon of onion powder

Directions

1. First, you place the pork chops in the slow cooker.
2. After which you pour the beans with their liquid on top.

3. After that, you add all other ingredients on top of that and stir the liquid and beans gently over the top of the pork to combine (make sure you do not stir the pork, just move the liquid and beans around to combine things a bit)
4. Then you cook on low for about 4-6 hours or until the pork easily breaks apart.

Slow Cooker Pork Tenderloin

NUTRITIONAL INFORMATION

Calories: 252

Points plus: 7

Fat: 0 g

Sodium: 816 mg

Carbohydrates: 15 g

Dietary Fiber: 0 g

Sugars: 13 g

Protein: 32 g

Ingredients

1 ½ - 2 pounds of lean pork tenderloin

Marinade:

1 tablespoon of Dijon mustard

1 tablespoon of lite soy sauce, low sodium (Tamari or Bragg Liquid Amino, optional)

2 teaspoons of freshly grated ginger

1 teaspoon of curry powder

Kosher (or sea salt to taste)

1 cup of chicken broth (fat-free, low-sodium)

1 tablespoon of rice wine vinegar

2 tablespoons of honey

2 cloves garlic (minced)

½ teaspoon of black pepper

Glaze: (it is optional)

2 tablespoons of lite soy sauce (or try BRAGG Liquid Aminos)

2 tablespoons of ketchup

1 tablespoon of Dijon mustard

2 tablespoons of honey

2 tablespoons of rice wine vinegar

1 tablespoon of sesame oil

Directions

1. First, you combine in a large mixing bowl all marinade ingredients.
2. After which you trim away all visible fat from tenderloin and discard.
3. After that, you cut tenderloin into 2" pieces and place in marinade, ensuring all sides are coated.
4. Then you cover and allow tenderloin to marinate overnight in the refrigerator.
5. At this point, you place tenderloin and marinade in slow cooker, cook on low for 4-6 hours, or until it shreds easily with a fork.
6. Furthermore, you remove from the slow cooker and place on a serving platter.

Direction on how to prepare glaze:

1. **First, you a**dd all ingredients to a small saucepan, bring to a boil, reduce heat to a simmer and cook about 5 minutes or until desired thickness.
2. Then you pour glaze over tenderloin.

Slow Cooker Pumpkin and Cranberry Topping

Minimum Slow Cooker size: 5 quarts

NUTRITIONAL INFORMATION

Serving Size: 1/2 Cup

Calories: 132

Points plus: 4

Fat: 5 g

Carbohydrate: 24 g

Dietary Fiber: 1 g

Sugars: 19 g

Protein: 1 g

Ingredients

2 teaspoons of pumpkin pie spice

1 teaspoon of pure vanilla extract

1 cup of fresh cranberries (diced)

1/3 cup of diced raw pecans

6 cups of uncooked pumpkin

1 cup of 100% orange juice

1/3 cup of raw honey

2 tablespoons of honey

½ teaspoon of cinnamon

Directions

1. First, you use an 8" whole pumpkin-- grown specifically for cooking, slice open and remove seeds and strings and cut pumpkin away from outer portion.
2. After which you cut pumpkin into 1" chunks and place in the slow cooker.
3. After that, you add pumpkin pie spice, orange juice, 1/3 cup honey and vanilla to slow cooker and stir to combine ingredients (make sure pumpkin pieces are well coated).
4. Then in a food processor, blender or by hand, dice whole cranberries.
5. Furthermore, in a small bowl you combine diced cranberries, 2 tablespoons honey, cinnamon and pecans.
6. Finally, you distribute cranberry mixture evenly over the top of the pumpkin, cover and cook on low for 4 to 6 hours.

Slow Cooker Pumpkin Butter

NUTRITIONAL INFORMATION

Serving Size: 2 tablespoons

Calories: 43

Points plus: 1

Fat: 0 gm

Carbohydrates: 11 gm

Dietary fiber: 1 gm

Sugars: 9 gm

Protein: 0 gm

Ingredients

1/3 cup (100%) apple juice (with no sugar added)

¼ cup of maple syrup

1 teaspoon of ground ginger

¼ teaspoon of ground nutmeg

1 (about 15 oz.) can pure canned pumpkin (not pumpkin pie filling) OR 15 oz. freshly baked and pureed pumpkin

¼ cup of honey

1 ½ teaspoon of ground cinnamon

¼ teaspoon of ground cloves

Directions

1. First, you stir all ingredients together in a 1 or 1 1/2 quart slow cooker and cook until it thickens (about 5-6 hours) on low.
2. Then while hot, it will still be runny, even after thickening.
3. After that, you place in a heat-safe container and chill overnight in the fridge.
4. Feel free to add more honey for sweetness if desired.

NOTE: remember that this is a "spicy" pumpkin butter.

If you want a milder version, I suggest you simply cut the ginger, cloves and nutmeg in half. (Feel free to add them back in later)

You can store in fridge for up to about 2 or 3 weeks (Freezes well).

Slow Cooker Rosemary Potato Soup

NUTRITIONAL INFORMATION

Serving Size: 1/2 Cup

Calories: 72

Points plus: 2

Fat: 1 gm

Sodium: 100 mg

Carbohydrates: 12 gm

Dietary fiber: 1 gm

Sugars: 1 gm

Protein: 3 gm

Ingredients

4 cups of low sodium chicken broth (I prefer the Imagine brand)

1 tablespoon of garlic powder

Salt to taste (this will need salt.)

4 medium russet potatoes (cooked and peeled, I microwaved mine till soft), and cut in to chunks.

4 low sodium vegetable bouillon cubes (I prefer the Rapunzel brand here)

2 tablespoons of onion powder

1 tablespoon of fresh rosemary, chopped + extra to taste (I prefer an extra 2 tablespoons)

Directions

1. First, you place everything in your slow cooker, EXCEPT THE ADDITIONAL ROSEMARY AND SALT, and cook on low for 2-4 hours.
2. Remember that by now the potatoes are already cooked, so the real purpose of cooking this is to get the bouillon cubes dissolved and to get all the flavors to meld, which a slow cooker does wonderfully.
3. Make sure you don't cook this too long, as the flavor of the potatoes will change.
4. Then when you're done cooking, use a hand blender to blend everything right in the slow cooker until smooth.
5. Furthermore, you can also transfer small amounts at a time to a regular blender (NOTE: a hand blender is MUCH easier and far less messy).
6. After which you blend in the extra rosemary and some salt to taste.
7. After that, you allow to cool and enjoy.
8. Finally, you serve with a piece of whole grain bread and a side of chicken breast!

Slow Cooker Southern Style Green Beans

NUTRITIONAL INFORMATION

Serving Size: ½ Cup

Points plus: 1

Calories: 37

Fat: 1 gm

Sodium: 101 mg

Carbohydrates: 6 gm

Dietary Fiber: 2 gm

Sugars: 1 gm

Protein: 2 gm

Ingredients

1 yellow onion (diced)

1 tablespoon of freshly chopped basil

2 pounds of fresh or frozen snap green beans (rinsed and strings removed)

Kosher (or better still sea salt to taste)

2 tablespoons of extra-virgin olive oil

2 cloves garlic (minced)

1 teaspoon of black pepper

1 medium potato (peeled, diced)

3 cups of vegetable broth (or better still chicken broth), low-sodium, fat-free

Directions

1. First, you sauté in a medium skillet onion and garlic on medium-low heat for about 4 minutes until tender.

2. After which you add sautéed onion and garlic along with all other ingredients to the slow cooker (**NOTE**: I recommend you use a 5-7 quart slow cooker).
3. After that, you cover and cook on low for 8 hours.

NOTE: Cooking time may vary depending on how tender you like your green beans (Southern style green beans are typically cooked until they are falling apart).

Slow Cooker Spicy Barbecued Chicken

NUTRITIONAL INFORMATION

Serving size: 2 drumsticks

Calories: 365

Points plus: 9

Fat: 14 g

Sodium: 140 mg

Carbohydrates: 28 g

Dietary fiber: 2 g

Sugars: 24 g

Protein: 32 g

Ingredients

8 drumsticks, with skin removed (3 split breasts or better still 6 thighs, optional)

Ingredient for the Barbecue Sauce

1 sweet onion (finely diced)

1 (about 8 ounce) can tomato sauce

¼ cup of balsamic vinegar (I prefer using white balsamic vinegar for gluten free)

1 tablespoon of Red Hot Sauce (I used 'Frank's Red Hot' in this recipe)

Sea Salt (to taste)

1 tablespoon of canola oil

1 clove garlic (minced)

¼ cup of honey

1 teaspoon of Dijon mustard

½ teaspoon of cayenne pepper

2 teaspoons of chili powder

Ingredients for the Spice Rub

1 teaspoon of dried oregano

1 teaspoon of chili powder

1 teaspoon of paprika

Sea Salt (to taste)

1 teaspoon of chipotle Chile pepper

1 teaspoon of cumin

1 teaspoon of ground mustard

1 teaspoon of black pepper

1 teaspoon of cayenne pepper

Directions

1. First, you add canola oil in a medium sauce pan.
2. After which you turn to medium-low heat and sauté onion and garlic for about 5 minutes until tender.
3. After that, you add the remaining barbecue sauce ingredients, stir and simmer for about 30 minutes until sauce has thickened.
4. Then while the sauce is cooking down, you combine spice rub and coat all sides of drumsticks.
5. Furthermore, after sauce has cooked down and thickened, you place drumsticks in the slow cooker, pour barbecue sauce over and ensure all drumsticks are covered.
6. Finally, you cover, turn to high and cook approximately 3 hours or until cooked through. Or, in the other way round, turn slow cooker to low and cook for about 5-6 hours.

Slow Cooker Spicy Sweet Potato & Bean Soup

NUTRITIONAL INFORMATION

Serving Size: 1 cup

Calories: 267

Points plus: 6

Fat: 5 g

Sodium: 433 mg

Carbohydrates: 49 g

Dietary Fiber: 11 g

Sugars: 10 g

Protein: 8 g

Ingredients

1 tablespoon of extra-virgin olive oil

4 medium carrots (peeled and sliced into 1/2" pieces)

1 cup of vegetable juice (optional tomato juice)

1 cup of canned lite coconut milk

½ teaspoon of cumin

1 teaspoon of freshly grated ginger

1 sweet potato (medium)

1 onion (diced)

1 (about 15 ounce) can Great Northern Beans

2 ½ cups of vegetable broth

½ teaspoon of crushed red pepper flakes

½ teaspoon of black pepper

Kosher (or better still sea salt to taste)

Directions

1. Meanwhile, you heat oven to 400 degrees.
2. After which you wrap sweet potato in foil, place on an oven safe pan and bake for about an hour until tender.
3. After that, you allow to cool slightly before peeling.
4. Then in a medium skillet, you add oil and sauté onion over medium-low heat for approximately 5 minute until tender.
5. Furthermore, you add onion, sweet potato, and all other ingredients to the slow cooker, stir to combine.
6. After that, you cover and cook on low for 6-8 hours, or high 3-4 hours.

For the Stovetop version:

1. First, you follow the instructions above except add ingredients to a heavy pot, bring to a boil over medium-high heat, reduce heat to a simmer and cook for approximately two hours until carrots are tender.
2. After that, you add additional broth or water for a thinner soup consistency.

Slow Cooker Spinach and Mozzarella Frittata

NUTRITIONAL INFORMATION

Serving Size: 1/6 of entire recipe

Calories: 139

Points plus: 4

Fat: 8 g

Carbohydrates: 4 g

Fiber: 1 g

Sugars: 2 g

Protein: 12 g

Ingredients

½ cup of diced onion

3 eggs

2 tablespoons of 1% milk

¼ teaspoon of white pepper

1 (packed) cup of chopped baby spinach (with stems removed)

Salt to taste

1 tablespoon of extra virgin olive oil

1 cup 2% of shredded mozzarella cheese (divided)

3 egg whites

¼ teaspoon of black pepper

1 Roma tomato (diced)

Directions

1. First, you add oil in a small skillet, and sauté onion on medium heat for about 5 minutes until tender.
2. After that, you lightly spray the inside of the slow cooker with nonstick cooking spray (I prefer to make my own by filling this reusable cooking spray bottle with olive oil or canola oil).
3. After which combine in a large bowl the sautéed onion, 3/4 cup mozzarella cheese, and remaining ingredients; whisk to combine, and pour into slow cooker.
4. At this point, you sprinkle remaining ¼ cup cheese on top of egg mixture.
5. Then you cover, and cook on LOW for 1–1 1/2 hours, or until eggs are set and a knife inserted in the center comes out clean.

Slow Cooker Sweet Potato Mash

NUTRITIONAL INFORMATION

Serving Size: 1/2 Cup

Calories: 111

Points plus: 3

Fat: 0 gm

Sodium: 63 mg

Carbohydrates: 26 gm

Dietary Fiber: 3 gm

Sugars: 8 gm

Protein: 2 gm

NOTE: This data does not include the pecans therein.

Ingredients

1 cup of apple juice (with no sugar added, 100% juice)

1 teaspoon of ground nutmeg

¼ teaspoon of ground cloves

2 lb. of sweet potatoes (peeled and cut into 1/2 inch slices)

1 tablespoon of ground cinnamon

½ teaspoon of allspice

AFTER COOKING, ADD:

Apple juice

Honey or better still maple syrup to taste (it is optional for those who like a sweeter version)

Cinnamon and nutmeg to taste

Pecans, for topping (it is optional)

Directions

1. First, you prepare your sweet potatoes and place in slow cooker.
2. After which you add ½ cup of the apple juice (NOT the full cup) and your spices.
3. After that, you cook on low for about 4-5 hours, until potatoes are tender (I recommend you use 3-4 quart slow cooker).
4. Then when potatoes are fully cooked through, you use a hand blender, blend the sweet potatoes inside your slow cooker insert, adding the second ½ cup of juice.
5. Finally, you season with more cinnamon and nutmeg to taste.
6. At this point, you top with pecans and enjoy.

Tips: remember while this dish is yummy without the pecans, the pecans truly add the final touch. Unless you have a nut allergy, we highly recommend the pecans. Do not be afraid of the fat in pecans, for it is healthy fat and perfectly acceptable for Skinny eating.

Slow Cooker Turkey Loaf

NUTRITIONAL INFORMATION

Serving size: 1/6 recipe

Calories: 184

Points plus: 5

Total Fat: 4 g

Carbohydrates: 20 g

Dietary fiber: 3 g

Sugars: 11 g

Protein: 18 g

Ingredients

1 egg (slightly beaten)

½ cup of diced sweet red bell pepper

Kosher (or better still sea salt to taste)

1 teaspoon of dried oregano

1/3 cup of ketchup

1 pound of lean ground turkey (about 93% lean), chicken or ground beef will also work

½ cup of diced yellow onion

1 cup of whole grain bread crumbs (NOTE: whole wheat panko will also work)

½ teaspoon of black pepper

1/3 cup of tomato or better still vegetable juice (I recommend without refined sugar)

Directions

1. First, you combine in a large bowl all the above ingredients, except ketchup, and mix well.
2. After that, you lightly spray the bottom and sides of the slow cooker with nonstick cooking spray (I fill this reusable cooking spray bottle with canola oil or olive oil).
3. Then you shape mixture into a loaf and place in the slow cooker (NOTE: You may need to reshape, just a bit, after placing in the slow cooker).
4. At this point, you cover and cook on low for 5-6 hours.
5. Furthermore, you add ketchup to the top about 30 minutes before the end of cooking time (I recommend you use 5-7 quart slow-cooker).

Slow Cooker Turkey Stew

NUTRITIONAL INFORMATION

Serving Size: 1 Cup

Calories: 183

Points plus: 4

Fat: 4 g

Carbohydrates: 17 g

Dietary Fiber: 4 g

Protein: 21 g

Ingredients

½ cup of diced onion

1 cup of sweet potato (peeled and cut into 1" cubes)

½ teaspoon of black pepper

½ teaspoon of crushed red pepper flakes

2 cups of chicken broth (fat free, low sodium)

1 - 2 pounds of leftover turkey or better still chicken pieces, chunks or shredded turkey will work

1 stalk celery (diced)

2 cloves garlic (minced)

2 carrots (peeled and sliced)

¼ teaspoon of cayenne pepper (more or less to taste)

1 cup of frozen peas

1 (about 14.5 oz.) can fire roasted tomatoes

Kosher (or better still sea salt to taste)

Directions

1. First, you add all the above ingredients, except turkey to the slow cooker, stir to combine.
2. After that, you cover and cook on low for about 8 hours or until carrots are tender.
3. Then you add leftover turkey, the last 30 minutes of cooking time and cook until heated through.

Slow Cooker Turkey Stroganoff

NUTRITIONAL INFORMATION

Serving size: 1 cup

Calories: 235

Fat: 9 g

Points plus: 6

Sodium: 252 mg

Carbohydrates: 17 g

Dietary fiber: 1 g

Sugars: 3 g

Protein: 21 g

Ingredients

1 mild onion (diced)

1 cup of chicken broth (fat free, low sodium)

1 tablespoon of balsamic vinegar

Salt (to taste)

2 tablespoons of cornstarch (if you prefer a thicker sauce I suggest you add it)

1 pound of lean ground turkey

4 ounces of mushrooms (button or baby Bella, sliced)

3 tablespoons of tomato paste

½ teaspoon of black pepper

1 cup of Greek yogurt (low-fat)

Directions

1. First, you add ground turkey in a large skillet and cook until it loses its pink color, drain off any fat and add to the slow cooker.
2. After that, you add extra virgin olive oil to the same skillet and sauté mushrooms and onions over medium-low heat for about 6 minutes until tender.
3. After that, you add the remaining ingredients to the slow cooker, except yogurt and cornstarch.
4. Then you cover and cook on low for 4-6 hours.
5. At this point, you combine Greek yogurt with cornstarch, add to stroganoff and continue cooking 30 minutes.
6. Finally, you serve over whole wheat egg noodles or brown rice.

NOTE: remember that this recipe can easily be adapted to be made in a skillet.

7. After which you cook the turkey and onion, drain and return to the skillet.
8. Then you add the remaining ingredients, except yogurt and cornstarch, stir and cook approximately 30 minutes.
9. Finally, you add yogurt and cornstarch, stir and cook until thickened.

Slow Cooker Winter Vegetable Medley

NUTRITIONAL INFORMATION

Serving Size: 1/2 cup

Calories: 128

Points plus: 3

Fat: 1 g

Sodium: 641 mg

Carbohydrates: 28 g

Dietary Fiber: 3 g

Sugars: 17 g

Protein: 4 g

Ingredients

2-1/2 cups of peeled and chopped butternut or better still acorn squash

1 teaspoon of thyme

Chopped chives or parsley (it is optional), for garnish

2-1/2 cups of baby carrots

1 onion (sliced)

2-1/2 cups of vegetable broth

½ teaspoon of sea salt

Directions

1. First, you put all of the ingredients in a slow cooker pot.
2. After which you cover and cook over low heat for about 4-6 hours, until vegetables are very tender.
3. Then you top with chopped parsley or chives, if using.
4. Finally, you serve with your favorite protein.

Slow Cooker Zucchini Ziti

NUTRITIONAL INFORMATION

Serving Size: 3/4 Cup

Calories: 272

Points plus: 7

Fat: 7 g

Sodium: 376 mg

Carbohydrates: 38 g

Sugars: 7 g

Dietary Fiber: 5 g

Protein: 15 g

Ingredients

3 cups (uncooked) of whole grain ziti shells (optional penne)

2 cups of mozzarella cheese (shredded)

¼ teaspoon of black pepper

½ cup of finely grated Parmesan cheese

1 (about 25 oz.) jar marinara (with no sugar added)

2 cups of fat-free cottage cheese

1 large zucchini (about 1/4" slices)

Kosher (or better still sea salt to taste)

Directions

1. First, you combine in a medium bowl the cottage cheese, mozzarella, and spices.

2. After which you add one cup marinara to bottom of the slow cooker.
3. After that, you combine (uncooked) pasta shells with remaining marinara.
4. Then you layer pasta coated marinara, zucchini, and cheese mixture until all ingredients have been used (NOTE: Cheese should be the last ingredient you add).
5. Finally, you cover and cook on low for two hours, or until pasta is al dente (I recommend you use a 5 to 7 quart slow cooker).

Spicy Chili with Fire-Roasted Tomatoes

NUTRITIONAL INFORMATION

Serving size: 1 cup

Calories: 212

Fat: 4g

Carbohydrates: 23g

Fiber: 6g

Protein: 16g

Ingredients

1 small yellow onion (diced)

1 (about 15-ounce) can organic kidney beans, (drained)

1 (about 14 1/2-ounce) can diced fire-roasted tomatoes

2 tablespoons of chili powder

½ teaspoon of red pepper flakes (or to taste)

Salt to taste

1 pound of lean ground beef

2 cloves garlic (minced)

1 (about 15-ounce) can organic black beans, drained

1 (about 6-ounce) can tomato paste

½ teaspoon of black pepper

1 ½ cups of water

Directions

1. First, you cook ground beef, diced onions, and minced garlic in a large skillet over medium heat, breaking up meat with a fork.
2. After which you cook until the beef has lost most of its pink color.
3. After that, you drain off fat and place in the slow cooker along with the remaining ingredients.
4. Then you cover, and cook on LOW for about 6-8 hours.

Slow Cooker Momma's Roadhouse Chili

NUTRITIONAL INFORMATION

Serving Size: 1 cup.

Points+: 6

Calories: 272

Total Fat: 7 gm

Sodium: 183 mg

Carbohydrates: 36 gm

Dietary Fiber: 13 gm

Sugars: 6 gm

Protein: 19 gm

Ingredients

2 small sweet onion

2 (15 ounce each) can black beans (drain)

2 (6 ounce each) can tomato paste

1 teaspoon of black pepper

1 teaspoon of crushed red pepper flakes

6 cups of water (for a thicker chili, I suggest you use 5 cups)

2 pound lean ground turkey, about 93% lean (it is optional, lean ground chicken or beef)

4 can (30 ounce) can kidney beans, drain

2 (14.5 ounce each) diced tomatoes

5 tablespoons of chili powder

2 teaspoons of Kosher or sea salt

2 cups of tomato juice (or better still veggie juice)

Directions

1. First, you cook turkey and onion in a skillet on medium heat, breaking up into small chunks.
2. After which you cook until no longer pink.
3. After that, you drain off fat and discard.
4. Then you add cooked meat and all other ingredients to slow cooker.
5. Furthermore, you cook on low for 6-8 hours.
6. I recommend you use 4-6 quart slow cooker.
7. Finally, you add diced onions and cheddar cheese, if desired.

Slow Cooker Thai Curry Ground Beef
NUTRITIONAL INFORMATION

Serving Size: ¼ recipe.

Points+: 5

Calories: 223.2

Fat: 8.7g

Carbs: 8g

Fiber: 1.6g

Protein: 25.2g

Ingredients

2 medium leek (sliced thin)

2 teaspoons of minced ginger

1 ½ cups of tomato sauce

2 tablespoons of soy sauce (make sure you use gluten free for Paleo and Gluten Free diets)

4 teaspoons of lime juice

2 lb. ground beef (93% lean)

4 garlic cloves (minced)

2 teaspoons – 2 tablespoons of red curry paste

2 teaspoons of lime zest

1 cup of light coconut milk

Directions:

Option 1:

1. First, you brown the ground beef and then add to the crockpot with the red curry paste, leek, garlic, ginger, tomato sauce, soy sauce, lime zest.
2. After which you cook on low for about 4 hours.
3. After that, you open the lid and stir in the coconut milk and lime juice.
4. Then you let cook for about 15 minutes longer and serve.

Option 2:

1. First, you heat a skillet over medium heat and spray with cooking spray.
2. After which you add the leeks and cook for about 4 minutes.
3. After that, you add the beef, garlic, and ginger and cook until beef is no longer pink.
4. Then you stir in the curry paste and cook for 1 minute.
5. Furthermore, you add the tomato sauce, lime zest, and soy sauce.
6. At this point, you turn the heat down to low and simmer for about 10 minutes.
7. Finally, you stir in the coconut milk and lime juice.
8. Then you let cook for 2 more minutes.

Slow Cooker Apple Cinnamon Oatmeal

NUTRITIONAL INFORMATION

Serving Size: 1 cup.

Points+: 5

Calories: 205

Fat: 3g

Carbs: 38g

Fiber: 5g

Protein: 7g

Ingredients

1 teaspoon of ground cinnamon

Pinches of salt

Enough water to fill Slow Cooker about ½ of the way full

Unrefined sweetener of choice (to taste)

1 cup of old fashioned (not quick cooking) oats

1 teaspoon of vanilla extract

4 cups of water

1 small apple (chopped)

Directions

1. First, you stir together in a small heat-proof bowl (that can hold at least four cups of water), the oats, cinnamon, vanilla, and salt. (Note: the apples can also be added in here).
2. As for me, I prefer to keep mine out to stir in after cooking, but this is up to you.

3. After that, you pour four cups water over oats.
4. Then you fill Slow Cooker about 1/4 to 1/2 of the way full with water (this will depend on the size of your Slow Cooker).
5. Furthermore, you add the heatproof bowl with the oat mixture to the Slow Cooker.
6. However, the bowl with the oats/cinnamon/vanilla has water in it, and also sits in the slow cooker surrounded by water.
7. Remember that the water level should rise almost to the top of the bowl.
8. At this point, you turn Slow Cooker on low for about 7-8 hours overnight.
9. In addition, you use a large spoon, remove bowl from Slow Cooker (note: it will be very hot!).
10. Finally, you stir in chopped apple and sweetener of choice.

Slow Cooker Balsamic Chicken

NUTRITIONAL INFORMATION

Serving Size: 1 cup.

Points+: 4

Calories: 190

Fat: 6g

Carbs: 5g

Fiber: 1g

Protein: 26g

Ingredients

2 (14.5 oz.) can diced tomatoes

4 garlic cloves

1 tablespoon of olive oil

Ground black pepper and salt (to taste)

4-6 boneless, skinless, chicken breasts (about 40 ounces)

1 medium onion thinly sliced (**NOTE**: Not chopped)

½ cup of balsamic vinegar (for gluten-free, I suggest you use White Balsamic Vinegar which doesn't have caramel coloring)

1 teaspoon of each: dried oregano, basil, and rosemary

½ teaspoon of thyme

Directions

1. First, you pour the olive oil on bottom of slow cooker.
2. After which you add chicken breasts, salt and pepper each breast, put sliced onion on top of chicken then put in all the dried herbs and garlic cloves.
3. After that, you pour in vinegar and top with tomatoes.
4. Then you cook on high for 4 hours, serve over angel hair pasta.

Slow Cooker Balsamic Chicken Wrap

Ingredients

2 tablespoons of prepared pesto (with no sugar added)

Leftover pieces of Balsamic Chicken

2 tomato and herb wrap

2 handful of baby spinach leaves

Directions

1. First, you place wrap on plate, spread with prepared pesto.
2. After which you add spinach leaves and top with chicken.
3. Then you wrap, slice in half and enjoy.

Slow Cooker Bananas Foster

NUTRITIONAL INFORMATION

Serving Size: ½ cup.

Points+: 4

Calories: 110

Fat: 2 g

Carbohydrates: 28 g

Dietary fiber: 2 g

Protein: 2 g

Ingredients

6 tablespoons of honey

½ teaspoon of cinnamon

2 tablespoons of coconut oil, melted (unrefined coconut oil)

Juice from 1 lemon

1 teaspoon of 100% Rum Extract (it is optional)

10 bananas, medium firmness, 1/2" slices

Directions

1. First, you add and combine the first four ingredients to the slow cooker.
2. After which you add banana slices, toss gently to coat with honey mixture.
3. After that, you cover and cook on low for about 1 ½ to 2 hours.
4. Then you add rum extract to bananas and stir to combine.

Directions if you using Stovetop Method:

1. First, you combine the first 4 ingredients in a medium saucepan.
2. After which you add banana slices, toss gently to coat with honey mixture, cover and cook on low heat for approximately 30 minutes, or until heated through and bananas are soft but not falling apart.
3. After that, you add rum extract and stir to combine.
4. Then you can enjoy alone or over favorite desserts.

Slow Cooker Beef Curry

NUTRITIONAL INFORMATION

Serving Size: ¾ cup.

Points+: 4

Calories: 176

Total Fat: 5 g

Sodium: 313 mg

Carbohydrates: 5 g

Dietary Fiber: 1 g

Protein: 28 g

Ingredients

4 teaspoons of curry powder

4 cloves garlic (minced)

1 teaspoon of black pepper

1 cup of freshly chopped cilantro

2 tablespoons of cornstarch or arrowroot + 2 tablespoons of water (optional)

2 pound lean stew meat (cut into bite size pieces)

2 small sweet onion (diced)

4 teaspoons of freshly grated ginger

Kosher or sea salt to taste

3 ½ cups of beef broth or stock (low-sodium)

Directions

1. First, you place stew meat in slow cooker.

2. After which you sprinkle with curry powder.
3. After that, you add all other ingredients and stir to combine.
4. Then you cover, cook on low for about 7 to 8 hours.
5. Remember, beef Curry is delicious served over a bed of brown rice, quinoa or couscous.
6. I recommend you cook on a 4- 6 quart slow cooker and for a thicker curry, I suggest you combine starch and water, add to slow cooker the last 15 minutes of cooking time.

NOTE: If preferred, I suggest you sauté onion in 2 tablespoons of olive oil for about 4 minutes until tender.

After which you add garlic and sauté one additional minute.

Then you add to slow cooker along with other ingredients.

Slow Cooker Beef Machaca
NUTRITIONAL INFORMATION

Serving Size: 4 oz.

Calories: 157.1

Fat: 4.4g

Carbs: 3g

Fiber: .8g

Protein: 24.9g

Ingredients

Salt and pepper

4 tablespoons of fresh lime juice

1 cup of red bell pepper (diced)

3 Serrano chiles (stemmed, seeded, and minced)

½ teaspoon of dried oregano

3 pound of beef brisket (or better still lean rump roast, trimmed of fat)

2 tablespoons of Maggi sauce (a Latino seasoning) or better still 2 tablespoons of Worcestershire sauce

1 ½ cups of diced onion

3 garlic cloves (minced)

½ cup of beef broth

½ (14 oz.) can diced tomatoes with juice

Directions:

1. First, you season the beef with salt and pepper and place into the slow cooker.

2. After which you whisk together in a medium bowl, the lime juice, beef broth, and Maggi.
3. After that, you stir in the other ingredients and then pour over the beef.
4. Then you cook on low in the slow cooker for about 8 hours.
5. At this point, you shred the beef using two forks and serve.
6. As for me, I usually like to let the shredded beef hang out in all the cooking liquid/sauce for about 30 minutes before serving. Make sure you keep the slow cooker on low.

Honey Mustard Pork Roast

Tip:

Remember, if you want to use more than five ingredients, I suggest you add baby carrots or some thickly sliced, peeled apples along with the onions and garlic.

Ingredients

4 cloves garlic (minced)

1 teaspoon of salt

1 teaspoon of dried thyme leaves

¼ cup of chicken broth

¼ cup of water

1 onion (chopped)

1/3 cup of honey mustard

¼ teaspoon of pepper

One (3 lb.) rolled boneless pork roast

1 Tablespoon of cornstarch

Preparation

1. First, you place onions and garlic in 4-6 quart crockpot.
2. After which you season pork roast with salt and pepper, and sprinkle with thyme.
3. After that, you spread honey mustard on roast.
4. Then you place coated roast on top of onions and garlic; add chicken broth.
5. At this point, you cover crockpot and cook on low for about 7-8 hours.
6. Furthermore, you remove roast and cover with foil to keep warm while making sauce.
7. After that, you combine cornstarch and water in a medium saucepan and blend with wire whisk.

8. In addition, you add juices and cooked onions and garlic from crockpot to saucepan and cook over medium heat until mixture boils and thickens, stirring frequently.
9. This is when you season to taste.
10. After which you add more salt, pepper, thyme, or honey mustard if needed (note: crockpot mutes these flavors because of its long cooking time).
11. Finally, you serve roast with sauce.
12. However, if you have a new hotter crockpot, I suggest you check the roast at 6 hours.

NUTRITIONAL INFORMATION

Serving Size: 1.

Calories: 250

Fat: 10g
Sodium: 390 mg

Lemon Feta Vinaigrette

NUTRITIONAL INFORMATION

Serving Size: 2.5 tbsp.

Points+: 2

Calories: 82

Fat: 8.3g

Carbs: 0.7g

Fiber: 0g

Protein: 18g

Ingredients

4 tablespoons of reduced fat crumbled feta cheese

2 teaspoons of Dijon mustard

½ teaspoon of garlic powder (or preferably 1 teaspoon of minced garlic)

4 tablespoons of lemon juice

2 tablespoons of extra virgin olive oil

1 teaspoon of dried oregano

Salt and pepper

If you like things creamy? I suggest you add 2-4 tablespoons of yogurt or reduced fat sour cream

Directions:

1. First, you add the lemon juice, feta, and olive oil to a small bowl.
2. After which you gently mash the feta using the back of a fork or spoon.
3. After that, you add the remaining ingredients and stir.
4. Then you taste and season with salt and pepper.

Many Bean Crockpot Soup

Tip:

Feel free to make this easy crockpot recipe using any mixed bean blend and just four other ingredients.

Make sure you use Hearty Bean Soup Mix for this delicious recipe.

Ingredients

2 onions (chopped)

1 teaspoon of dried thyme leaves

14 oz. of can diced tomatoes (undrained)

2-1/4 cups of Hearty Bean Soup Mix (without seasoning packet, or mixed dried beans)

10 cups of water (or better still chicken broth)

4 carrots (chopped)

Preparation

1. First, you combine all ingredients except for tomatoes and stir well to combine.
2. After which you cover crockpot and cook on HIGH setting for about 8-10 hours or until beans are tender.
3. Then you add tomatoes, stir, cover, and cook on high for 15-20 minutes longer until heated.

Mexican Crockpot Pork

Tip:

Remember that tender chunks of pork loin are slowly cooked with chunky salsa and some pinto beans in your crockpot.

Make sure you serve this recipe for Mexican Crockpot Pork over fried slices of prepared polenta.

Ingredients

4 cups of chunky salsa

1 teaspoon of dried oregano leaves

½ teaspoon of salt

4 pounds of boneless pork roast (cut into 2" pieces)

30-ounce can pinto or better still black beans (rinsed and drained)

¼ teaspoon of pepper

Preparation

1. First, you mix all ingredients in 4-5 quart slow cooker and cover.
2. After which you cook on low for about 6-7 hours until pork is tender.
3. If you'd like a thicker mixture, I suggest you mix 4 tablespoons cornstarch with ½ cup water and add to the crockpot.
4. Then cover and cook on low 10-15 minutes until thickened.

NOTE: for newer, hot crockpots you cook on low for about 4-1/2 to 5-1/2 hours until pork registers 155 degrees F.

Orange Roast Pork

TIP:

Remember that frozen orange juice concentrate is the secret ingredient to provide sweetness and lots of flavor in this easy four ingredient crockpot recipe.

Ingredients

1 onion (chopped)

¼ cup of brown sugar

¼ teaspoon of pepper

2 Tablespoons of cold water

1 (about 3-1/2 lb.) pork shoulder roast

6-oz. can of frozen orange juice concentrate

1 teaspoon of salt

2 Tablespoons of flour

Preparation

1. First, you trim roast of visible fat.
2. After which you place onions in bottom of 3-4 quart crockpot.
3. After that, you sprinkle salt and pepper over roast and place in crockpot on top of onions.
4. At this point, you mix together in small bowl, thawed orange juice concentrate and brown sugar, and salt and pepper, and pour over roast.
5. Then you cover crockpot and cook on high for about 3 hours, then reduce heat to low and cook for another 3 hours.
6. Furthermore, you remove roast and onions from crockpot, cover, and set in low oven to keep warm.
7. After which you skim fat from juices in crockpot and then pour into large heavy pan.
8. In addition, you blend flour and cold water in small bowl and add to juices in pan.
9. Then you bring to a boil and cook, stirring frequently with wire whisk, until thickened.
10. Finally, you serve gravy with roast and onions.

Overnight Slow Cooker Pumpkin Pie Steel

Cut Oats: With No Sugar Added

NUTRITIONAL INFORMATION

Serving Size: 1 cup.

Points+: 2

Calories: 188

 Fat: 1g

Sodium: 193 mg

Carbohydrates: 15 g

Dietary Fiber: 2 g

Sugars: 7 g

Protein: 1 g

Ingredients

7 cups of water (NOTE: almond or regular milk can be substituted)

2 teaspoons of vanilla extract

2 teaspoons of pumpkin pie spice

2 cups of steel cut oats

2 cups of canned pumpkin puree

½ teaspoon of salt

It is optional: 1 cup of honey or better still 4 teaspoons of vanilla liquid stevia

NOTE: Sweetener can be added during cooking or cook it without and each person can add their own sweetener of choice on top after cooking.

Directions

First, you combine all ingredients in your slow cooker and cook on low for 8 hours.

Enjoy!

Red Potatoes with Caviar and Cheese Recipe

Tip:

You can cook this potatoes in the microwave or baked in the oven.

Remember that this classy side dish is both low-calorie and low fat.

Ingredients

3 Tablespoons of Neufchatel cheese

1 Tablespoons of black lumpfish caviar

12 new red potatoes (about 1 pound), scrubbed

1 Tablespoons of low-fat (1 percent) buttermilk

1 teaspoons of chopped dill

Preparation

1. First, you place the potatoes in a single layer in a shallow microwavable container.
2. After which you cook on high for about 3 minutes until fork-tender.
3. Alternately, bake the potatoes at a temperature of 350 degrees for 20 minutes.
4. After that, you cut the potatoes in half; place, cut-side down, on a platter.
5. Then with the help of a spoon or a melon baller, make a small well in the top of each potato.
6. Furthermore, you mix in a small bowl the cream cheese and buttermilk until smooth.
7. Then with the help of a rubber spatula, fold in the dill and caviar.
8. Finally, you dollop about 3/4 teaspoon of the mixture into the well of each potato.

NUTRITIONAL INFORMATION

Serving Size: per serving.

Points+: 1

Calories: 54

 Fat: 1g

Carbs: 10g

Protein: 2g

Salsa Crockpot Chicken

Tip:

Feel free to use any flavor of your favorite salsa in this super easy and delicious recipe. (For me, I like the complex sweet and hot flavor of fruit salsas in this recipe).

The smaller grocery stores are carries fun flavors of salsa.

You can serve it with Chili Rice Casserole to soak up the wonderful sauce.

Ingredients

6 pounds boneless, skinless chicken thighs

2 (16 ounce each) jar peach salsa

Preparation

1. First, you combine in a 3-4 quart crockpot and cook on low for about 6-8 hours, until chicken is tender and thoroughly cooked.
2. After which you can leave the lid off the crockpot.
3. Then you cook it on high for the last 30-45 minutes to thicken if you'd like, or mix 4 tablespoons cornstarch with ½ cup water and add that; cook 20-30 minutes longer on low.
4. However, this can also be made with chicken breasts; cook on low for about 4-6 hours until the chicken is done.

Saucy Crockpot Beef

Tip:

Make sure you serve this rich and delicious savory Saucy Crockpot Beef recipe with a creamy sauce over hot mashed potatoes or hot cooked rice.

The last time I made this, I added a chopped onion and some minced garlic.

Ingredients

2 (10 ounce) can condensed cheddar cheese soup

4 pounds beef stew meat (OR better still sirloin steak, cut into 1" cubes)

4 (10 ounce) cans condensed tomato soup

Preparation

1. First, you place meat in the crock pot and then pour the soups over the meat and mix well to combine.
2. After which you cover slow cooker and cook for 8 to 10 hrs. Until meat is tender.
3. Then you stir well and serve over hot cooked rice or noodles.

Savory Crockpot Short Ribs

Ingredients

1 teaspoon of pepper

2 cups of barbecue sauce

1 teaspoon of dried thyme

1 teaspoon of paprika

8 lbs. of beef short ribs

24 oz. of jar beef gravy

2 lb. of frozen bell peppers and onions (thawed and drained)

1 teaspoon of dried basil

Preparation

1. First, you place in 3-4 quart crockpot ribs and sprinkle with pepper.
2. After which you mix in medium bowl, gravy and barbecue sauce and pour over top.
3. After that, you cover crockpot and cook on low for about 9-11 hours until beef is tender.
4. This is when you skim fat from surface of liquid in crockpot.
5. Then you add bell peppers, onions, herbs, and paprika to slow cooker and cover and cook on high 40-50 minutes until hot.
6. Finally, you serve vegetables and sauce with ribs.

Crockpot Poached Salmon

Tip:

Make sure you cook salmon to tender, moist perfection in your crockpot or slow cooker.

However you should vary the seasonings according to your own tastes if you'd like.

Ingredients

4 tablespoons of lemon juice

1 teaspoon of salt

8 cloves garlic (minced)

1 teaspoon of dried dill weed

8 salmon steaks

2 cups of water

¼ teaspoon of white pepper

2 onion (sliced)

4 tablespoons of butter

Preparation

1. First, you grease the bottom of a 3-4 quart slow cooker and stack the salmon fillets in the appliance.
2. After which you combine remaining ingredients in a heavy saucepan and bring to a boil over high heat.
3. After that, you stir, then pour over salmon in crockpot.
4. Then you cover and cook on low for about 3-1/2 hours or until salmon flakes when tested with a fork

Shredded Asian Beef

NUTRITIONAL INFORMATION

Serving Size: 4 oz.

Points+: 4

Calories: 169.4

Fat: 5g

Carbs: 3.8g

Fiber: .7g

Protein: 24.8g

Ingredients

½ cup of soy sauce

¼ cup of brown sugar

2 tablespoons of sesame seeds

It is Optional: 1-3 teaspoons of Asian chili sauce

1-2 jalapenos (seeded and minced)

3 lbs. of beef eye of round or better still bottom round roast, all fat trimmed

¼ cup of rice wine vinegar

2 tablespoons of ketchup

1 inch ginger (minced or grated)

8 cloves garlic (whole)

½ red onion (minced)

Directions:

1. First, you whisk together in a bowl the soy sauce, brown sugar, vinegar, ketchup, ginger, sesame seeds, and hot sauce if you are using it.
2. After which you stir in the onion, jalapenos, and garlic cloves.

3. *After that, you place beef in the slow cooker and pour the sauce over the beef.*
4. *Then you cook on low for 8 hours until beef is fork tender.*
5. *Finally, you shred and let hang out in the crock pot for about 30 minutes more for all the juices to combine.*

Slow Cooker Beef Ragu

NUTRITIONAL INFORMATION

Serving Size: ¾ cup.

Calories: 175.8

Fat: 5.4g

Carbs: 3.8g

Fiber: 9g

Protein: 27.4g

Ingredients

1 ribs celery (diced)

1 carrot (peeled and diced)

1 (about 14.5 oz.) can diced tomatoes

1 ½ cups of beef broth

Salt and pepper

2 tablespoons of fresh oregano or thyme (chopped)

2 ½ pounds of lean beef chuck (trimmed of fat)

1 onion (diced)

4 garlic cloves (minced)

1 (about 14.5 oz.) can crushed tomatoes

2 bay leaves

2 tablespoons of fresh rosemary (minced)

Directions:

1. First, you add the carrots, celery, onion, and garlic to the bottom of the crock pot.

2. After which you season your beef liberally with salt and pepper and add it to the crock pot.
3. After that, you add the remaining ingredients and cook for about 6-8 hours until beef is fork tender.
4. Then you serve with your favorite pasta, or polenta, or even in sandwiches for an Italian beef sandwich.

Slow Cooker Butter Chicken

NUTRITIONAL INFORMATION

Serving Size: ¾ cup.

Points+: 6

Calories: 240.1

Fat: 13.8g

Carbs: 5.1g

Fiber: 7g

Protein: 24.7g

Ingredients

2 tablespoons of vegetable oil

½ white onion (chopped)

4 teaspoons of lemon juice

2 inch ginger (minced)

2 teaspoons of chili powder

2 bay leaves

½ cup of half and half

2 cups of tomato sauce

2 pinches of black pepper

4 lbs. of chicken breast (cubed)

2 shallot (finely chopped)

4 tablespoons of butter

8 garlic cloves (minced)

4 teaspoons of garam masala

2 teaspoons of ground cumin

½ cup of plain nonfat yogurt

1 ½ cups of skim milk

4 ½ teaspoons of cayenne pepper (or to taste)

2 pinches of salt

Directions:

1. First, you heat the oil in a medium sauce pan, over medium heat.
2. After which you add the shallot and onion and sauté until soft.
3. After that, you add the ginger, garlic, butter, lemon juice, garam masala, cayenne, chili powder, cumin, and bay leaf and cook for 1 minute until fragrant.
4. Then you add the tomato sauce and cook for 2 minutes stirring often.
5. In addition, you add the half and half, milk, and yogurt.
6. After which you reduce heat to low, stir, and simmer for about 10 minutes.
7. At this point, you stir frequently.
8. This is when you take a taste and season with salt and pepper.
9. Furthermore, you add everything to a blender and blend until well combined.
10. Finally, you add cubed chicken breast to the slow cooker and cook for 4 hours.
11. You can enjoy it better with rice or cauliflower rice.

Slow Cooker Butternut Squash Soup

Minimum Crock Pot size: 5 quarts

NUTRITIONAL INFORMATION

Serving Size: 1 cup.

Points+: 4

Calories: 174

Total Fat: 1 g

Sodium: 162 mg

Carbohydrate: 36 g

Dietary Fiber: 9 g

Sugars: 4 g

Protein: 8 g

Ingredients

3 potatoes (scrubbed and cubed)

1 cup of white corn (optional: yellow corn)

1 (about 15 ounce) can white beans (rinsed and drained)

1 onion (diced)

1 teaspoon of cilantro (or 1 "bunch" fresh cilantro)

½ teaspoon of ginger

1 jalapeño, diced (it is optional)

3 cups of butternut squash (cubed)

1 bell pepper (diced)

1 (about 15 ounce) can black beans (rinsed and drained)

1 (about 14.5 ounce) can diced tomatoes

2 cups of vegetable or better still chicken broth (preferably low sodium, low fat)

½ teaspoon of cayenne pepper

¾ teaspoon of cumin

½ teaspoon of ground black pepper

Directions

1. First, you combine all ingredients in slow cooker.
2. After which you cover and cook on low for about 6-8 hours.
3. However, for added color and flavor, I suggest you sprinkle with a small amount of fresh cilantro and a fresh shaved parmesan.
4. This recipe is best served with jalapeño cornbread.
5. To make, I suggest you add one diced jalapeño to your favorite cornbread recipe

Slow Cooker Carnitas

NUTRITIONAL INFORMATION

Serving Size: ¾ cup.

Points+: 6

Calories: 224.9

Fat: 7.7g

Carbs: 1.3g

Fiber: .1g

Protein: 25.8g

Ingredients

1 onion (diced)

¾ teaspoon of salt

1 teaspoon of oregano

1-2 diced chipotle peppers and 2 tablespoons of adobo sauce

1-2 bay leaves

2 ½ lbs. of pork shoulder (lean only, trimmed of fat)

3-4 garlic cloves (minced)

½ teaspoon of pepper

1 teaspoon of cumin

¾ cup of light beer (or better still chicken broth)

Directions:

1. First, you season the pork with salt and pepper.
2. After which you place it in the crockpot.

3. After that, you mix together the remaining ingredients in a bowl and pour over the pork.
4. Then you cook for about 6-8 hours on low until the pork is fork tender and easily shreds.
5. In the meanwhile, you heat the oven to a temperature 500 degrees.
6. At this point, you lay pork out in a single layer on a non-stick baking sheet.
7. Finally, you roast for about 4-5 minutes until the edges become crispy and toasted.

Slow Cooker Cheesy Spaghetti with Turkey Sausage

NUTRITIONAL INFORMATION

Data using turkey sausage:

Serving size: 1-1/4 cup

Calories: 372

Points plus: 9

Fat: 13 g

Sodium: 175 mg

Carbohydrates: 38 g

Sugars: 9 g

Fiber: 6 g

Protein: 25 g

Data without turkey sausage:

Serving Size: 1 cup

Calories: 289

Points plus: 7

Fat: 9 g

Sodium: 142 mg

Carbohydrates: 38 g

Fiber: 6 g

Sugars: 9 g

Protein: 15 g

Ingredients

1 (about 24 ounce) jar spaghetti sauce (with no sugar added)

1 cup of low fat cottage cheese

1 cup of low-fat ricotta cheese

1 tablespoon of chopped (fresh) basil or better still 1 teaspoon of dried basil

½ teaspoon of ground black pepper

1 lb. of lean ground turkey sausage

8 ounces (uncooked) 100% whole wheat spaghetti (of about 2/3 of a 13.25 oz. box, break into small pieces before adding to meat mixture)

1 cup of skim mozzarella cheese (shredded)

1 teaspoon of dried oregano

Kosher or sea Salt to taste

Ingredients to Make Turkey Sausage

½ teaspoon of garlic powder

1 teaspoon of dried sage

1 teaspoon of dried oregano

1 lb. Of lean ground turkey or preferably chicken

½ teaspoon of freshly ground black pepper

¼ teaspoon of cayenne pepper

Directions

1. First, you add all the sausage ingredients a large mixing bowl and mix thoroughly.
2. After which you cook ground turkey sausage in a large skillet over medium heat, breaking into small pieces while cooking.
3. Make sure that the turkey loses its pink color before removing from heat.
4. After that, you drain, discard any fat and set aside.
5. At this point, you combine meat with marinara.

6. Furthermore, you combine in a medium bowl, the cooked turkey sausage with the remaining ingredients, add to slow cooker.
7. After that, you cover and cook on low 2 hours until cheese is bubbly.
8. Then you add spaghetti and ¾ cup of water, stir thoroughly and cook for an additional hour until the spaghetti is cooked through.
9. Finally, you serve and sprinkle with parmesan if you wish.

Slow Cooker Chicken and Mushroom Gravy

NUTRITIONAL INFORMATION

Points+: 6

Calories: 261

Fat: 10 g

Dietary Fiber: 2 g

Sodium: 462 mg

Carbohydrates: 9 g

Sugars: 3 g

Protein: 34 g

Ingredients

4 tablespoons of oil (I prefer canola)

2 yellow onion (thinly sliced into rings)

1 teaspoon of black pepper

½ cup of fresh flat leaf parsley (chopped)

4 tablespoons of cornstarch

3 pounds of chicken breast filets (about 6 filets), skinless

32 ounces crimini mushrooms (sliced)

4 cloves garlic (minced)

Kosher or sea salt to taste

3 cups of chicken broth (preferably low sodium, fat free)

Directions

1. First, you add oil to a skillet or slow cooker, but if you using a Stovetop Slow Cooker, turn to medium-high heat and sear chicken on both sides just until brown.
2. After which you remove and place on a paper towel.
3. After that, you reduce heat to medium-low, add onion to the same skillet, and sauté for about 4 minutes until tender.
4. Then you add chicken, onion and remaining ingredients to the slow cooker.
5. Cover and cook on low 3-1/2 to 4-1/2 hours or until chicken is done and easily flakes with a fork.

Note: onion, mushrooms and garlic go on top of chicken.

6. Furthermore, you remove chicken from slow cooker and set aside.
7. At this point, you add cornstarch to slow cooker and whisk until smooth.
8. In addition, you return chicken to slow cooker and continue cooking for about 15 minutes until gravy is thick.

TIP: when you add the onion to the skillet, I suggest you pour in about a ½ cup broth to deglaze the pan and pick up all the bits on the bottom of the pan from the chicken and then add to the slow cooker.

Serving suggestions: you can serve over brown rice or whole wheat pasta.

CONCLUSION

Thanks for reading through this book; if you follow judiciously the recipes outlined above, you will sleep better, feel better, think better, have more energy and loss weight without effort.

Remember, the only bad action you can take is no action at all.

THANK YOU.

If you enjoyed the recipes in this book, please take the time to share your thoughts and post a positive review with 5 star rating on Amazon, it would encourage me and make me serve you better. It'd be greatly appreciated!

Thank you and good luck!

www.ingramcontent.com/pod-product-compliance
Lightning Source LLC
Chambersburg PA
CBHW081723100526
44591CB00016B/2482